a lc

modern
badass

TALES FROM THE
LEADERSHIP FRONT

parissa behnia

The Sixense Empathy Model™ is a trademark of Parissa Behnia
The Values-Velocity Matrix™ is a pending trademark of
Parissa Behnia

ISBN-13: 978-1-957651-21-7
Library of Congress Control Number: 2022920005

Designed by Rachel Valliere of Printed Page Studios

INDIE BOOKS INTERNATIONAL®, INC.
2511 WOODLANDS WAY
OCEANSIDE, CA 92054

www.indiebooksintl.com

Contents

Preface. vii

CHAPTER 1:

In Praise Of "Too Much" 1

What Makes Someone A Modern Badass? 4
Consistency Is Key 7
The Elephant In The Room 8
Aesop's Fable Of Androcles And The Lion 9

CHAPTER 2:

Confessions Of A Modern Badass. . . 11

Know Your Own Strength 15
Choose Velocity Over Speed 16
The Intersection Of Light And Dark 17
The Edgy Serves A Purpose 18
Negative Space Defines Opportunity 20
Cracking The Code 21

CHAPTER 3:

Make Friends And Influence People . 23

There's No Prize Above Grand Prize. 25
Declare Your Vision, Share Your Purpose 27
Choose Velocity, Not Speed. 28
Why Bother? 32

CHAPTER 4:

Keeping Your Modern Badass
Volcano Dormant 35

Oops, I Did It Again 36
Take A Stroll Down Memory Lane 37
Putting Insights Into Practice. 40
The Values-Velocity Matrix 41
Resist The Urge To Assume People Will Follow 43
It's A Marathon, Not A Sprint 45

CHAPTER 5:

Meet People Where They Are 47

Clarity, Like Sunlight, Is The Best Disinfectant 48
Create A Goal GPS. 50
A Goal GPS Template 50
Yes, Be Present 52
Dollars And Cents 53

CHAPTER 6:

Vulnerability Is Not A Four-
Letter Word. 55

Be Seen As Human 56
Lead With Courage. 58
Bluffing Only Works In Poker. 61

Sixense Empathy Model 63
The Crocodile Of Invulnerability Is Always Hungry . . 64

CHAPTER 7:

Congratulations, You're Human 67

Be Seen As Human 68
Rip Off The Band-Aid 69
Actually, Love Does Mean Having To Say You're Sorry 70
Embrace Internal Disruption 71
Try Uncertainty On For Size 72
Stop Being Chief Executive Of Everything 74
Dare Mighty Things 75

CHAPTER 8:

Lather. Rinse. Repeat. 77

Getting In A Lather. 78
Growth Mindset Is Your Friend 79
The Power Of Yet 82
You Might Be Resistant. 83

CHAPTER 9:

The Goldilocks Effect 85

You Define Your Leadership In Each Moment. 86
What Is Required Of You. 87
You Might Regress 89
Your Legacy Is Calling 91

CHAPTER 10:

Hugging A Cactus. 93

You Have An Invitation To Blossom 94
What's At Stake. 94
How Does This Get Done? 95
A State Of Being 98

Appendix 99

Acknowledgments. 101

About The Author 103

Notes 105

Preface

This is my manifesto. My name is Parissa and I am a business whisperer.

I help leaders and businesses discover and unleash their superpowers, the stuff that defines *their* brilliance. My absolute favorite thing is to stand in front of whiteboards with my clients and ask, "What could the world look like if we created/explored/tested?"

I love creativity and ambiguity. I love pushing past what we believe our limits may be. I love disruption and pattern interrupts. I love change agents and being messy and edgy. Actually, I *really* love being messy and edgy.

I serve clients. I don't please them.

I don't care about how the donuts are made. I trust some soul whose Zone of Genius is donut-making will take care of that. I care about making new fantastic and tasty donut recipes with my clients that amaze their clients. That's my Zone of Genius.

We're all brilliant diamonds. My brilliance is serving yours, and I'd like to help you channel yours.

How badly do you want to shine?

This book is my love letter to each and every modern badass out there.

Parissa Behnia
Chicago, 2022

IN PRAISE OF "TOO MUCH"

Have you ever been told that you are "too much"? I have.

This book is a love letter to modern badasses. They are high-performing senior leaders and startup founders going eighty miles per hour in a forty-five mile per hour zone who don't always check to see if their teams (or clients) are strapped in for the ride, let alone interested in going to that destination.

They are pattern interrupters, creative change agents, and innovators who usually ask, "Why not?" instead of asking, "Why?" They don't "make the donuts" so much as make new donut recipes. They have audacious goals in mind that make people look at them in both fear and awe, separately and simultaneously. They are of high value to any company, whether their own or someone else's.

They love creativity and ambiguity. They love pushing past what the rest of us believe our limits may be. They love disruption. They love being messy and edgy. They really love being messy and edgy. That's practically another food group.

They are like well-meaning bulls in a china shop. They are creators at heart and don't mean to break as many dishes as they do, but the fact is that they do break dishes. Frequently. But let's face it, a lot of that china was ugly and out of date anyway.

How are modern badasses typically described? These labels may seem familiar to you: bold, aggressive, colorful, creative, innovative, brash, loud, difficult to manage, disruptive, contrary, etc.

Most people think it's better to ignore or sideline this type of leader. It's tempting to treat them as if they were lepers rather than trying to connect or engage with them. The truth is, modern badasses can have an outsized impact on all of us when they create new ways to engage and enroll clients, peers, and teams instead of repelling them. They have the capacity to be seen, heard, understood, and respected for who they are as opposed to hiding themselves and playing a smaller game to suit someone else's taste.

No, this isn't putting all the responsibility on them—they aren't broken or need to change. There are three sides to every story: one, the other, and the truth. The blame game is easy to play by believing that the person on the other side of the table needs to change to suit you. They don't. What is available to everyone, modern badass or not, is the ability to create new ways to be seen, heard, understood, and respected; this is a matter of choice.

Modern badasses include Sara Blakely, Ida B. Wells, Ruth Bader Ginsburg, Steve Jobs, Thomas Edison, Shonda Rhimes, Harriet Tubman, Sunny Bonnell, Ashleigh Hansberger, Madame CJ Walker, Shirley Chisholm, John Lewis, Martin Luther King Jr., Banksy, Grant Achatz, Susan B. Anthony, Wolfgang Amadeus Mozart, Muhammad Ali, Kasia Urbaniak, Alexander Hamilton, Lt. Gen. Russel Honoré (retired), Reshma Saujani, Ray Kroc, Sepideh Nasiri, Shannon Downey, Wangari Maathai, and many others.

Not attracting or enrolling others comes with a cost. In its ongoing "State of the American Workplace" report, Gallup shows us that employees leave leaders, not jobs or companies. And there are a number of great books and significant articles in the *Harvard Business Review* and other journals that talk about the hard and soft costs of bad and ineffectual leadership. Now is the time to have this conversation about creating strong leaders and stronger relationships.

Why me? Time for a confession: I'm one of you. I'm a modern badass.

What Makes Someone A Modern Badass?

There are fourteen traits I've uncovered in my work as a coach and advisor to modern badasses.

You know your bright side and embrace your dark side. These days, we hear quite a bit about strengthening our strengths, also known as your bright side. Makes perfect sense. However, modern badasses are aware of and embrace their dark sides too. You understand *the dark side has value*, and can be tamed and leveraged to your advantage.

There's no crying in baseball. It's an awesome quote from an entertaining movie, *A League Of Their Own*. It applies to badass leaders too, because they face adversity head-on. You can get frustrated by unexpected outcomes (um, you are human), but you've never counted yourself out. You have a ton of courage and grit.

You sometimes feel lonely. You have super high standards for yourself and others. The problem is that you've never shared how much harder you are on yourself than on the people around you. You've never shared how often your negative highlight reel gets replayed in your head and the words you use to punish yourself for your failures. That means you've alienated yourself (unintentionally, of course).

You crave connection with people. You can leap tall business goals in a single bound and yet want to feel like you have your crew. You want a community with people who champion and challenge you because they think so much of you but you don't always know how to create that community. The loneliness you may feel is like a leg shackle you would like to break.

You know how to FITFO. Modern badasses always figure it the flip out. If you can't solve something one way, you solve it another way. You live for challenges and puzzles—the more complex, the better. You have a love-hate relationship with being stumped by something.

You are super creative. There's nothing better than standing in front of a whiteboard and asking, "What is the opportunity for us here?" You see new possibilities and solutions better than many of your peers. The idea of possibility gets you excited every single time without fail.

You have Spidey sense. Your intuition is off the charts. Your "knowing" is a gift you leverage regularly. And when you remember to use it with your IQ, no one can stop you or anyone who works with you.

You suffer from self-doubt. You're objectively one of the most talented people around, but you frequently suffer from imposter syndrome. You keep asking yourself if you have what it takes to continue to propel forward.

You are a disruptor. You challenge norms. You don't make the donuts so much as you make new donut recipes. You're not afraid to tell it like it is, and you're not scared to interrupt patterns. You don't disrupt for disruption's sake though. You direct your energy toward helping your team and clients get to where they need to go.

You have a quick wit. Your humor is sharp, sometimes wicked. You have a keen sense of the absurd, which helps you overcome challenges as they may present to you. You can be working the hardest you have ever worked, and yet you can find something to laugh about too.

Your loyalty game is off the charts. You stick your neck out for things you believe in: your business, your team, your clients, and your values (especially your values). You know your people can fend for themselves, but you take leadership responsibility seriously. Their peaks and valleys are your peaks and valleys too.

It's hard for you to ask for help. Being independent is a double-edged sword. You get a lot of stuff done on your own, but it's really hard for you to receive help even though you know that pride comes before a fall.

You keep it real. You're easily bored. And it's patently obvious when you're bored. You can't phone it in as other people do. Your dissatisfaction is evident if you're reeled into work you're not passionate about. If you're not passionate about it, you want no part of it.

You sometimes go eighty miles per hour in a forty-five mile per hour zone. You're so passionate about the things that engage you that you press the pedal all the way down. You feel awesome when your team is with you, but often your engine is much stronger than the team's engine. They may not know the destination or may not be interested in it.

Consistency Is Key

A contradiction is one of the most frustrating things for these leaders to experience. On the one hand, they're looked to be that high-value, high-performing leader: that creator, that innovator, that visionary, that disruptor, etc. And yet on the other hand, it can sometimes feel like they're being told that while the powers that be want all of those things, the badasses have to change, have to conform, have to be other than who they are at their core. It can feel like rejection. It can feel like they are being sidelined. The temptation can be to just double down, consequences be damned. And sometimes the consequences are damning.

How damning? It makes many people think these leaders do not care about how they affect others and aren't interested in playing nice in the proverbial company sandbox. But what's true is that these leaders crave connection with others but don't always know how to co-create it. The more disconnecting, disruptive moments can live as a negative highlight reel on constant repeat in their minds.

The good news is that there's another way. You can be that badass leader *and* create a connection without compromising your values or fundamentals. Badass leaders can and do create ways to enroll and engage others on a shared, larger goal. It's not redemption as they've committed no crime. Instead, this is about a deeper and more meaningful understanding that becomes available to all of us.

The Elephant In The Room

There is a subset of modern badasses who are rather intense. Some people may call them jerks or use blue language to describe them. I call them "3D" leaders (difficult, dismissive, and divisive). They have a habit of turning everything into gold but leaving collateral damage behind. So they are still of high value but they tarnish their value the more their behavior goes unchecked.

Let's be abundantly clear that 3D leaders do *not* include narcissists, toxic leaders, or predators. They aren't people like Vishal Garg, the CEO of Better.com, who laid off nine hundred employees on Zoom right before Christmas 2021; he accused them of "stealing" from colleagues and customers by being unproductive and only working two hours a day. He apologized for the damage his action had done the next day but it was too late.

Adam Neumann, the former WeWork CEO, isn't a 3D leader either. He could not crystallize a path to WeWork profitability despite millions of dollars worth of outside investments. Perhaps more egregious than wasting money, he demonstrated numerous instances of poor executive judgment, e.g., borrowing from the company while also charging rent for properties he owned, putting relatives in positions of power, etc.[1]

The invitation to you is to see a 3D leader's humanity and not sideline or dismiss them out of hand, particularly during the times when they are unable to articulate their own humanity and vulnerability. These people have a lot to offer us once we choose to stop treating them in 2D.

Aesop's Fable Of Androcles And The Lion

Do you remember Aesop's story of Androcles and the Lion?

Once there was an escaped slave named Androcles who ran into the forest to get away from the guards chasing him. In his desperate search for a hiding place, he came upon what looked like a fearsome lion, which made him turn tail (pardon the pun) and head in the opposite direction. And yet, something about the lion made Androcles turn around and approach. As he got close, the lion extended his paw, which was swollen and bleeding. Androcles soon saw a thorn that was the cause of the lion's pain. He removed the thorn and wrapped the lion's paw so it would heal. Afterward, the lion took care of Androcles and brought him meat daily to live.

The story goes on about Androcles' and the lion's eventual capture and how Androcles' sentence for escaping was a public spectacle in an arena. His punishment was to be thrown to the very same lion he healed and befriended for the lion to kill. The lion was released into the arena, where it ran in and roared while hunting for its prey. The lion stopped in its tracks because it recognized Androcles. Instead of attacking, he fawned over him.

This book isn't about changing who you are, whether you are a modern badass or a 3D leader. You can't turn a mighty lion into a docile sheep. It's just not possible. What you can do is to remove the thorn, much like Androcles removed the lion's thorn. This book is about working on yourself and with others to remove the thorn together and channel your awesomeness.

If anyone has ever said working with you was like "hugging a cactus," I celebrate you. If anyone has told you that you were "too much," I applaud you. If you've felt less than because you believed you were "too much," I honor you. I celebrate you if you've ever chosen to play a smaller game because you were tired of hearing "too much" and being alienated.

It's not that modern badasses are "too much," but we have not created the conditions and the environments where we present in the best light. So instead of having our genius sidelined by being told we're too disruptive, bold, brash, etc., let's create hearing and knowing that we're "just what the doctor ordered."

2

CONFESSIONS OF A MODERN BADASS

Modern badasses are always well-intentioned. They're super passionate and excited to create their next adventure and bring people along for the ride. Sometimes, however, modern badasses can be like over-torqued spark plugs. When they're over-torqued, they unintentionally cause stress or damage. Candidly, they can suffer more damage than those around them because they harbor such regret over how others have felt in their midst.

Trust me. I know.

My name is Parissa Behnia and I'm both a modern badass and a 3D leader. Earlier in my career, I kept on living up to the definition of insanity often misattributed to Einstein: I did the same things over again and expected different results. Every. Single. Time.

What did I do? I'll give you an example.

Earlier in my corporate life, I was told I was the hardest person my leader ever had to manage. It was so hurtful and confusing to me because until that point, I felt like my mission to drive business results meant being creative, testing limits, trying new things, and maybe breaking old rules to make new ones. I felt like I was on the hook to rattle some cages.

Now, I am not a victim and take full responsibility for my behavior. If my job description was in the shape of a square, for example, I'd always want to turn it into a triangle, a sphere, or whatever caught my fancy. I felt compelled to question why the work I was doing couldn't be more than it was. And, you guessed it, that's where I bumped into the most resistance because I didn't appreciate the environment, timing, content, context, etc. I wasn't reading the room. I had way too much speed and not enough velocity.

At the time, what I heard in that "hardest person to manage" feedback was, "do all the disruption but don't do it in the way you're doing it because you're not right." In other words, I thought I was hearing "deliver all the numbers but don't be you." My individuality was not valued or welcome.

I'll never forget the moment I heard that, nor will I forget how that felt. It was, in short, devastating. It's also when I started to double down on being both a modern badass and a 3D leader (difficult, dismissive, divisive).

It doesn't matter if my being the hardest person to manage was or wasn't factually true. It was the truth to my leader. That was the only truth that mattered as the buck stopped with him when it came to a team that worked well together and delivered measurable business results to the company.

Here's how the feedback landed with me, which became my version of the truth for a very long time:

- You are contrary and not in a way anyone finds charming.
- You're broken and can't be repaired, coached, helped, etc.
- You are not valued.
- You do not belong.

So how did I live up to the earlier-cited definition of insanity? These are some actions that may be familiar to you.

I wasn't paying attention to my environment. I didn't have clarity on my key values, which are freedom, truth, justice, creativity, and loyalty, why they were my key values, or what would happen when I was out of alignment with them.

I kept trying to prove I was right instead of trying to become influential. I repeated the pattern of being the proverbial square peg trying to fit into that round hole, with the goal of being the first person to do that successfully.

I didn't know where my *home* was. I joined spaces that were always out of alignment with who I was as a person and with my values. I didn't know how to find the place where I felt included and yet still remained an individual.

I didn't have a personal advisory board. I didn't have a trusted circle of people to offer insight, support, and tough love to help me get out of my own way.

Hindsight is twenty-twenty, and there are no victims in my story, now or in the past. In my case, no one was ever the bad guy, so much as I wasn't aware and didn't know the importance of awareness. I didn't pay critical attention to the internal conditions I needed to create so I could shine consistently. I didn't pay critical attention to the external conditions out of my control that had to exist so I could shine consistently. Nothing was done to me so much as I had to learn how to give voice to who I was as a leader in a way that felt right to me and engaged others to join me on an adventure.

I've since realized three truths from that time I was told I was too difficult to manage:

- Leaders are not given the tools, guidance, training, or coaching to lead. They're just tossed into the deep end and expected to lead.
- I didn't know how to ask my leaders for the help, training, coaching, etc., that I needed.
- Leaders are not born in a vacuum-sealed container.

Leaders are born in exactly these moments I've shared. It's earlier in someone's career when, if we all had the awareness, training, and mindfulness, we could help and not hurt our leadership development, modern badass or not.

The good news is that you don't have to throw the baby out with the bath water. Modern badasses and 3D leaders can and do have a tremendous impact on their clients, teams, and peers. They can be and be seen as valuable disruptors and channel their awesomeness. *All. The. Time.*

Know Your Own Strength

We must recognize we don't know our own strength (or its impact). There's a funny US cartoon called *The Adventures of Rocky and Bullwinkle and Friends* that features Rocket J. ("Rocky") Squirrel and Bullwinkle J. Moose. One of the many ongoing gags in the cartoon series is that Bullwinkle pretends he is a magician and tells Rocky that he's going to pull a rabbit out of a hat. In one of the many attempts to pull the rabbit out of a hat, Bullwinkle pulls a rhinoceros out instead, about which he matter-of-factly says, "I don't know my own strength."

The cartoon gets a laugh every time someone sees it, but when it happens in real life, it's hard to find that humorous. We may think we're pulling a rabbit out of a hat to everyone's delight, but instead we get something that looks and feels like a fearsome rhinoceros on the attack. Having a handle on our own force and strength is very hard, sometimes painful, when we don't have the tools, guidance, training, or coaching.

Just as the lion became friends with Androcles, we can find a way to see the rhinoceros as something for the good.

Choose Velocity Over Speed

There's also something about moving too fast for the conditions.

There's velocity, and then there's speed; it's easy to believe they are the same thing but they're not. Velocity is the rate of travel in a given direction. Speed is the rate of travel. Velocity, for our purposes, is better than speed.

When we're like over-torqued spark plugs, however, it can feel and seem like speed and not velocity to others. That high rate of travel can be scary and alienating to other people if the destination isn't clear to them or why it may benefit them directly to join us for the ride. Scary and alienating kind of defeats the purpose of enrolling and engaging others to see the shared goal and get as excited about it as we are.

Speed over velocity has another problem too. When we go too fast, we're not sharing a little bit more of what drives us: our values. When we withhold that which is most dear to us, others don't see our content and context. They see something two-dimensional and believe we're rudderless, or that we fly off the handle easily and for no reason.

What's worse? If we fail to be curious about their values, they are hard-pressed to place faith or trust in us or care about our values. We don't create a community or a basis for understanding if we're not sharing our values or if we aren't asking people what their values are.

The Intersection Of Light And Dark

We have a gift for balancing our bright and dark sides. Let's look at the sun as a metaphor. We really appreciate it only when light and dark come together, like at sunset.

At sunset, you can see the pinks, purples, oranges, reds, yellows, blues, whites, etc. You're in awe of the display because you see how light and dark come together to create beauty. Sure, you like the light and warmth of the sun during the day, but you're not struck by the sun as much as you are at sunset.

Modern badass leaders are exactly the same way. You show your magic when your light and dark sides meet. You're not appreciated when you hide or camouflage the dark and only show the light in hopes that you will be found palatable to others or if you're afraid that you aren't welcome somewhere. That's a two-dimensional, manufactured, and superficial version of you. It's not believable and counterintuitively, it might be hard for others to trust you even though you think the camouflaging would help.

Your dark side can and does create magic when it meets your light side. Often.

Brené Brown, professor, researcher, author, and speaker, says,

> "Only when we are brave enough
> to explore the darkness will we
> discover the infinite power of
> our light."[2]

The Edgy Serves A Purpose

When working on a jigsaw puzzle, some people like to start with the outer edges and then work their way in. You don't look for the corner pieces because if you're working on a five-hundred-piece square-shaped puzzle, you'll be spending a lot of time looking for .8 percent of all the pieces, which is not at all the best use of your time. You also know it's not the best use of your time to start solving the puzzle from the middle either.

Many leaders are content to be in the middle. They deliver results consistently but they don't rattle cages, nor do they want to rattle cages. These leaders will do just enough for the bump in salary, a bonus, and a contribution to the 401(k) plan. Overall, it's not a bad strategy because it's comfortable to be in the middle, rather like the feeling you have when sitting in your favorite lounge chair. When you're content to be in the middle, the edges seem too out there, too far away. The risk seems just too high, so these leaders stay away from the edges because it may be too hard to calculate the upside. You've guessed it—the middle isn't where modern badasses ever like to be. For them, it's like a death sentence.

Modern badasses know the middle isn't where innovation lives. They intuitively know, and more importantly, feel it's a mistake to start from the milquetoast middle when pondering what's next. Badasses know innovation lives at the very edge of our limits. Consequently, they stay far away from the middle when they want to build products, strategies, etc.

The lessons modern badasses have learned time and again is that you need your edges just like you need air to breathe. The edges are vital because they define the space, idea, product, etc., you are creating. Even if edges aren't the subject, you see the subject clearly because of the edges. Your edges give you content and context. They help propel you forward.

Modern badasses know that starting and trying to stay in the middle is like a sugar high you must keep gorging on to avoid the crash. For them, it's better and easier to embrace the risk of being on the edge than it is to sustain the sugar high of the middle.

Sunny Bonnell and Ashleigh Hansberger support the idea that leaning into edgy serves a purpose when they wrote about the experience of developing Motto, their company, in their book *Rare Breed*: "We were doing things differently—breaking rules and vandalizing traditions. This was our identity, and we needed to own it. Instantly, we became more confident in tearing up the rule book, running our business on our own terms, and being who we were—not who we were supposed to be."[3]

The edges help you be who you are, not force you into a form of you that is sanitized and palatable for other people's sensibilities. They help you tear up the rule book much like Sunny Bonnell and Ashleigh Hansberger have done.

Negative Space Defines Opportunity

Negative space is an important fundamental of art. You've seen it before even if you didn't know its name. Simply put, it is the area around and between a subject so you see the subject more clearly. In some cases, the negative space is more interesting than the subject. For example, there's a famous black and white image that, when you look at it from one angle, is a young woman. But from another angle, it's an older woman. The FedEx logo is another popular example of negative space. Once you see the arrow in the FedEx logo, you can't unsee it. Negative space can be fun and whimsical.

Negative space is also fundamental to being a modern badass leader. There's never positive without negative. There's never light without dark. We need negative and positive as well as light and dark to see and capture opportunity. Light and dark allow you to see multiple angles and multiple perspectives.

It's tempting to want to stay in a positive space. But doing so means lacking balance, content, and context. The cost? Your innovation, your spirit, and your voice.

Modern badasses champion negative space because they know we can do better. They advocate for it as a means to go deeper into the heart of every matter.

Cracking The Code

We'll unlock the code to your success that will still allow you to be you while creating community, enrolling, and engaging others successfully.

3

MAKE FRIENDS AND INFLUENCE PEOPLE

It's great that you might be Superman. What people may need or want at key moments is Clark Kent instead. We all have this image of the superhero who leaps tall buildings in a single bound; we all have romantic versions of doing the same for our peers, clients, teams, etc.

Since disruptors like you are necessary in our world, there's beauty in knowing how much force to exert per situation and when to invite other people in to exert force with you or instead of you. You should know 110 percent of your sole effort is more disruptive to peers and teams than is often realized. Remember, Bullwinkle pulled a rhinoceros out of a hat because he didn't know his own strength. People are wired to help once when they've bought into an exciting idea *and* know how to deploy their brand of power to be of value to it.

There are people out there who can make things happen with you *and* they have the expertise you may not (gasp). That is a gift. What is not a gift is a compulsion to control a situation. Control is an illusion and is more about your insecurity and inability to temper it than directing to the desired outcome. It's easy to believe control is your friend, but the truth is you may be cutting yourself off from opportunity when you exert too much control.

There's a tendency with modern badasses to over-compete not only with other people but, more dangerously, with themselves. Growth mindsets are wonderful and everyone should lean into them. However, there is a danger of leaning into it so much that it feels like one-upping a colleague (or worse, a senior leader) instead of improvement for improvement's sake. Your intent doesn't matter because that's not taped to your forehead for others to see. Perception is reality, and so if you are perceived to embrace one-upmanship, you will turn people off. If you genuinely have an audacious goal, you need to hear people say "*hell yes*" and not "*hell no*" to what you envision.

> "Try not to become a man of success but rather to become a man of value."
> —Albert Einstein[4]

Clark Kent always knows he's Superman. And you always know you have the power to make things happen. It's tempting for a modern badass like you to believe you must make all the things happen all the time. Flying solo may be the worst thing you could do, even though you can technically do it on paper. The truth is you don't have to fly solo like Superman does.

Let's examine this further.

There's No Prize Above Grand Prize

Modern badasses are competitive because of their ambition, creativity, and excitement for what's next. This will be familiar to you if you're an Enneagram Type 3 or 8.[5] Enneagram 3s and 8s are order makers, not order takers.

In an interview with Hayden Lee[6], an International Coaching Federation Master Certified Coach and Enneagram specialist, he describes the Enneagram as a system of development that helps us understand *why* we do what we do, and our "core motivation" that drives our default patterns of thinking, feeling, and acting.

Lee explains the Enneagram consists of nine core motivation types. Each type has great strengths as well as potential pitfalls. Once you land on your core type, the real work begins to develop into the healthiest, most effective, most fulfilled version of your type.

Enneagram Types 3 and 8 often fall into the modern badass category because assertiveness, ambition, competition, drive, efficiency, goal orientation, and the ability to get things done quickly is in their DNA. However, any strength in excess becomes a weakness.

The core motivation for Type 3 is *the need to outshine the rest and be the best.* Enneagram 3s love everything about success: how to pursue it, achieve it, and look it. They set a goal and will do what it takes to achieve it. They value winning and are great at asking for what they want.

The core motivation for Type 8 is *the need to be strong, be in control, and avoid vulnerability.* Enneagram 8s are natural leaders who don't hesitate to take charge, love challenges and say what must be said, albeit bluntly. They're fiercely protective, especially of those who they see as needing protection.

Both 3s and 8s can be incredible assets to any team or organization until they're not. Those they lead may start to question their authenticity because they always seem to "be on" and charismatic, yet rarely show vulnerability or share their feelings.

Unhealthy 3s "win at all costs" attitude may cause them to cut corners, bend the truth, and make others feel that winning is more important than people and feelings.

Unhealthy 8s also avoid vulnerability to their detriment. They are very sensitive and generous with huge hearts, but showing a softer side of themselves is a rarity. They may present as too controlling, explosive, intimidating, and unapproachable. Their tough exterior and bluntness may cause others to feel run over, underappreciated, and in extreme cases, bullied. While 8s can move on quickly after expressing anger, it may take others time to recover from that experience.

Learning to become the healthiest version of you is liberating and can help you grow into your next level of badassery. You're not to embrace this for others so much as for your happiness.

Declare Your Vision, Share Your Purpose

People aren't mind readers. You're on the hook to declare your vision and share your purpose. Tell your clients, peers, and team what you're creating, why it's important, and why they are integral to achieving it. Your role as a visionary leader isn't solely to be a renegade. Your role also is to have a clear idea of what success looks like, recruit the best people who buy into the vision, and find the best resources to maximize your vision's impact.

Going it alone is your Kryptonite—Superman gets weak when exposed to Kryptonite. You lose your strength when you don't include others in your vision journey. You minimize your impact when you don't cast the net wide for brilliant ideas and brilliant people.

Here's a secret: People respect you more when you admit that you can't do it alone. It's courageous to ask for help and to admit you don't have everything you need to succeed. Permit yourself to say, "I need help to bring this to life."

Choose Velocity, Not Speed

Our teams, clients, and peers can handle high velocity, going at high rates of speed as long as they have bought into the goal you've described clearly. But if you've never shared, only half shared, or believed they could read your mind about the goal, they'll never accept the shared goal mission you have in mind, even if objectively it's in their best interest. It doesn't matter if you're right. They deserve to hear what you envision.

No one is obligated to do as you say, even when you know in every fiber of your being that what you have in mind benefits *everyone*. The onus is on you to make it easy for them to believe in and be a "hell yes" for the adventure. They need and want to believe it too. The onus is on them to step through the adventure door once you've opened it and invited them along for the ride.

Start by identifying and sharing values. How do we develop a shared belief in the goal? Since we've learned it's not by fiat (not the car), we've got to try another way. We enroll and engage others based on what our complementary (not identical) values might be.

But first, what are your values? They might be service, leadership, and personal growth. Or they might be freedom, truth, and creativity. Why are these values important to you? What happens when you feel like you might be out of alignment with your values? Are you low energy and less productive, or do you become irritable or resentful?

Here is a sample list of values to help you get started in identifying what is most important to you. Please note that this is in no way an exhaustive list. There are many other values you may identify with.

Accomplishment	Integrity
Achievement	Leadership
Adventure	Loyalty
Altruism	Nature
Autonomy	Openness
Commitment	Orderliness
Communication	Personal Growth
Community	Physical Appearance
Creativity	Power
Emotional Health	Privacy
Environment	Professionalism
Excellence	Recognition
Family	Respect
Flexibility	Romance
Freedom	Security
Friendship	Self-Care
Fulfillment	Self-Expression
Fun	Service
Holistic Living	Spirituality
Honesty	Trust
Humor	Truth

Then, step into some vulnerability and share your values. Share why they are important to you and why your values align with the goal. Be edgy and show your Achilles heel by telling others what happens when a conversation or situation is in misalignment with your values. That's typically where conflict and misunderstanding live. Sunlight is the best disinfectant, as Judge Louis Brandeis famously stated. When things are out in the open, you minimize the chance of conflict.

Get to a place of understanding. Your clients, peers, or team may have completely different values. Early on in any engagement or relationship, ask them to share the values most important to them and what happens to them when there's misalignment. Then invite them to explore how their values could be aligned with the goal. It is important to find complementary values between you so the goal can feel a little more exciting and engaging for *everyone*. By sharing your key values with others and asking them about theirs, you create content and context for the exciting goal you have together. You're co-creating depth and foundation.

Before this exploration gets discarded as a "waste of time," remember that every goal, project, or strategy has its peaks and valleys. It's very easy to collaborate when things are running smoothly. It's during the times when there are challenges or setbacks that conflicts occur. Knowing your key values upfront makes it easier to collaborate amidst a challenge or setback.

Remember, you're not trying to ask anyone to adopt your values, nor do you have to abandon what's important to you. You're meeting them where they are for mutual understanding, respect, and a commitment to the goal.

The goal becomes much easier to achieve if everyone has skin in the game. And you might even exceed your vision of success.

> "When people know what they are playing for, they naturally want to outperform what they are playing for."
>
> —*Carla Harris, Morgan Stanley's vice chair, global wealth management, and senior client advisor*

It's easy to fall back into your Superman habits. Resist the urge. No one badasses quite the way you do. It's easy for you to say, "I'll just do this myself because it's much easier than trying to explain what I want," or "No one can do this as well or as fast as I can." That's been your winning strategy to date, and you have a ton of success to show for it. But, as they say, what got you here won't get you there.

Remember, there's no prize above the grand prize. There are only so many times you can over-compete before people tire completely of you, think you're unserious, and believe you're just showboating. You might have the best ideas that will benefit everyone but if no one listens, your ideas will be in vain.

> "The flame that burns twice as bright burns half as long."
> —Lao Tzu, Te Tao Ching

You have more impact by serving others, not focusing on an arbitrary finish line. Trust yourself enough to engage meaningfully with others. Let them know the values that drive you so they can find that place of connection with you and what you're trying to achieve. Trust them enough to be hand-raisers for the goal and accept their expertise. Choose velocity, not speed.

Why Bother?

Yes, you are right frequently. You've got the track record to prove it. At this point, to prove you are right and remind others of all the other times you were right is churlish. Being right has nothing to do with the price of gold. What solely matters is the goal you want others to enroll and engage in for their benefit. If they're not enrolled or engaged, it doesn't matter that you've made some salient points.

As Jordan Goldrich wrote in his book, *Workplace Warrior: People Skills For The No-Bullshit Executive:*

In many corporations, businesses, and organizations, the top executives rightly see their responsibility as developing strategy. However, they often do not remember that creating alignment throughout the value chain is also their responsibility. In my experience, they may request input from an external consultant and several trusted internal stakeholders. But they often fail to systematically collect input from the entire value chain. Too often, input from the stakeholders closest to the customer is not seen as worth taking the time to collect. When, in fact, this input is often one of the keys to success.[7]

Simply put, your ego can kill your empathy. You lose objectivity and opportunity when you choose to make yourself the sole decisionmaker and are uninterested in the input of others. It's so tempting to believe it's always better to be Superman, not Clark Kent. The truth is the more you lean into being Superman, the less you find opportunity and a way forward. Also, you'll be less admired or seen as a valuable leader.

KEEPING YOUR MODERN BADASS VOLCANO DORMANT

Mount Vesuvius, the only active volcano in mainland Europe, is located on the west coast of Italy. In AD 79, it erupted and destroyed the cities of Pompeii and Herculaneum. The volcano is still considered dangerous today, given its proximity to the city of Naples, other surrounding towns, and the Amalfi Coast.[8]

What makes Vesuvius dangerous is that the African tectonic plate upon which it rests has a tear in it, meaning the heat from the earth's mantle can melt the rock of the African plate, subsequently building up pressure that causes an eruption.

This potential eruption is not unlike what can happen with modern badasses and 3D leaders if there's not been alignment on values and the shared goal. Like what happened in Pompeii, many badasses and 3D leaders can leave bodies in their wake.

Some may believe modern badasses and 3D leaders erupt without cause. The truth is that pressure and stress due to misalignment can build up over time and explode, like when two of the earth's tectonic plates cause a volcanic eruption. Our objective is to know what may cause pressure and stress to help head off any potential eruption. The more awareness we develop, the more effective we are as leaders.

Oops, I Did It Again

Sometimes, in the compulsion to pursue what you know is *right*, you accidentally choose speed over velocity. It's easy to mistake the two, especially when moving too fast for the conditions. The confusion is where (serious) conflict and misunderstanding can live unless you have some tools in hand to help you.

If you've ever driven in a snowstorm, you know how dangerous it can be because you don't see the ice underneath the snow. You might drive too fast or lose traction, and unless you're an expert driver, you might spin out. Experienced drivers understand you can't drive too fast for the conditions; otherwise, you'll end up in a ditch or worse.

The same is true with modern badasses. If you move too fast for the conditions, you can unintentionally cause damage to others, particularly the ones with whom you might be most eager to create a community. Once the damage is done, it takes great effort to make amends. You may have repelled some people, and it may take some time to get to reconciliation. Or worse, the damage is so bad that reconciliation is not possible.

The damage is something that lives as a negative highlight reel on constant repeat in your mind. You know there's nothing worse than adding to that reel. Consequently, you're judge and jury, and you're always convicted and sentenced without probation.

Your role as a visionary, that person who has an audacious goal, is to create the optimal conditions for velocity for everyone, not just you. Your role is to lead in achieving that goal, whether from the front, the side, or behind. Thus, any setback you experience is very costly. The good news is there are ways to help you design the optimal conditions so you can create and retain your community in service of the larger goal.

Take A Stroll Down Memory Lane

It seems simplistic, but it is often a matter of patience. Let's explore yours within the context of what you're trying to create for everyone's benefit. You don't take a half-baked cake out of the oven. The cake might not look or taste very good if you did. Taking a half-baked cake out of the oven might defeat the purpose of trying to make a cake in the first place. The same is true with your goals. They aren't achieved with a snap of a finger, mindreading, or brute force. They are achieved when aligned with values.

Modern badasses have a laundry list of the times when they have moved too fast for the conditions with poor results. Your intentions are good, and the excitement for the outcome usually is the cause for how fast you're moving. You forget to "slow your roll" and unintentionally create conflict. It's a hard habit to break because there are plenty of times that moving too fast for the conditions has worked in your favor. The more senior you are in an organization, however, the less successful that approach can be, especially when alignment with your colleagues or your team is a critical ingredient for success.

Think of an instance where you moved too fast or forgot to invite people to join you for the ride instead of assuming they were already buckled in. You may have pressed your foot down on the accelerator while they were still getting in the car. Think of what happened afterward: conflicts, misunderstandings, and setbacks.

Recount

1. What were the circumstances?
2. What was driving the rush and the urgency that you forgot to or couldn't or wouldn't communicate the goal with others?
3. What about the circumstances was misaligned with your values?

4. What were your physical signs that you were about to go eighty miles per hour in a forty-five mile per hour zone?
5. What was the larger point you missed because you left everyone behind?
6. What nuance did you miss because you left everyone behind?
7. What was the cost because you left everyone behind?
8. How did this impact others?
9. How did this impact you?
10. What could you have done or communicated differently?

Reflect

1. What insight have you gained from this instance?
2. What patterns do you see?
3. What effect does this insight and your noted patterns have on you upon reflection?
4. What can you do differently?

3D leaders also have a laundry list of the times they were like Mount Vesuvius. Because they can be difficult, dismissive, and divisive, they either disrupt or erupt, sometimes in legendary fashion, with each new episode cutting deeper than the last one. Recall a significant disruption or eruption of yours. Think of what happened afterward: reactions, setbacks, confusion, and misunderstandings.

Recount

1. What were the circumstances?
2. What about the circumstances was misaligned with your most important values?
3. What were the physical signs of discomfort you had before the eruption?
4. What was the more significant point you missed?
5. What nuance did you miss?
6. What was the cost of your eruption?
7. How did this impact others?
8. How did this impact you?
9. What could you have done or communicated differently?

Reflect

1. What insight do you have from this instance?
2. What patterns do you see?
3. What impact does this insight and your noted patterns have on you upon reflection?
4. What can you do differently?

Putting Insights Into Practice

How good are you at being "present" and in the moment? It's one of the hardest things for a badass like you to learn. You would be in excellent company if you were to admit you're terrible at being present and in the moment.

You can put your insights from the previous exercises into practice by being present to not only who you are in the moment but also to the people sitting at the table with you. Noting what happens in the moment is of *strategic importance* to you. You are presented with data and nuance that will help you make the best possible decisions to achieve your goal and establish understanding and connection with others. Your attention is a matter of choice. Alignment is also a matter of choice.

Mindfulness can be learned and incorporated into your life. Many apps, such as Calm and Headspace, can introduce you to mindfulness practice. The more you choose mindfulness, the more it presents in all moments, regardless of how much stress you may be experiencing.

The Values-Velocity Matrix

Now that you know how to uncover insights and put them into practice, you may find this matrix helpful to plot where you might be at any given moment with any given initiative.

The x-axis measures when you employ speed versus velocity. The y-axis is the continuum between aligned and misaligned values. There are four quadrants to this matrix.

Excellence. This is your happy place. You have a goal in mind that is aligned with your values, so you're employing velocity. Everything feels easy, even if you're working the hardest you've ever worked on something incredibly complex. You also have great collaborative efforts between you, your clients, and your team.

Expansion. This is your "I could be happier" place. What you're working on is aligned with your values but it appears to be rudderless because the goal isn't as well defined as it could be. The expansion invitation is to clarify the intent and why it matters so you can move into Excellence. If you can't get clarity on the goal or why it matters, it may be best to disengage until you find something that best suits you.

Exploration. This is your "I'm bored and phoning it in" place. What you're working on has a clearly defined goal, but there's nothing here that engages or excites you because it isn't aligned with your values. If you can't find alignment, it may be best to engage in something that feels like a better use of your time. You don't mind being a team player, but if it takes too much of your time and attention you may become restless or even resentful.

Explosion. This is your "I'm Mount Vesuvius erupting" place. There is no clearly defined goal you're working toward; you may find it hard to articulate one, or worse, the people with whom you work can't or won't articulate the goal. There's movement but not in a constructive direction. Adding insult to injury is that there is nothing about this work aligned with your values, or perhaps you haven't explored the complementary values you have with the people on your team. Combining speed with values misalignment is where you're most vulnerable to alienating your team and clients.

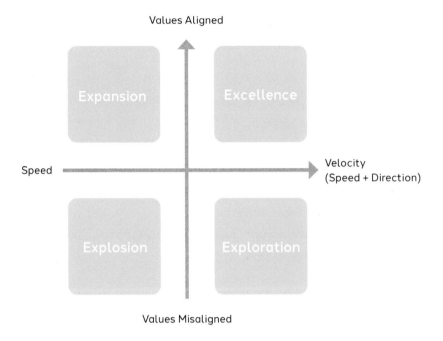

Resist The Urge To Assume People Will Follow

The temptation is great to leap ahead and assume people will follow because it just seems *easier* to do so or because you've already decided your approach is the best. Whether a sin of commission or omission, the outcome is practically signing the death certificate of what you're trying to accomplish. Resist the urge.

Consider these steps the next time you must have buy-in, contribution, or an endorsement. This could be in a meeting, in response to an email, or in a presentation to your board—these may seem like they take too long, especially if something needs to be done yesterday. The truth is that you can move through these speedily if you're *present* and in the *moment*.

1. Be present. Be clear on the objective in that moment.
2. Actively listen to hear what's being said and pick up nuance.
3. Actively listen to hear what's not being said and ask for clarification.
4. Activate your "high speed" or "eruption" alert checkpoint:
   a. Recall your values and watch for potential misalignment.
   b. Check for the physical signs you uncovered in the previous exercise. Notice your breathing and your heart rate, for example. Are they elevated?
5. Name it to claim it. Acknowledge a potential misalignment and ask clarifying open-ended questions to get to a place of understanding.
   a. *Who, what, which, when,* and *how* are the great question words we learned in elementary school.
   b. Avoid asking *why* questions as they create defensive postures in others. For example, ask, "What drives that conclusion?" instead of "Why do you conclude that?"
6. Be present to let conversation and ideas breathe to co-create solutions.

It's A Marathon, Not A Sprint

Practice. Practice. Practice. You're not going to get this right the first time. Maybe not even the second, either. This isn't about a one-time leadership performance or about heeding the call of the one-upmanship troll. What you are seeking is leadership mastery, which means iterative learning. If the goal is worth it to you and aligns with your values, commitment to practice will be easy.

Yes, it can be an uncomfortable experience and you won't be the only one to feel that way. Here's an incentive: committing to practice will help you stop adding to the negative highlight reel. You will get to the point where this work will be muscle memory and not an irritating checklist. You'll get so good and move through the practice so swiftly that you'll catch yourself in the moment if you're falling into past habits and can course correct on the spot.

5

MEET PEOPLE
WHERE THEY ARE

In Lewis Caroll's *Alice in Wonderland*, Alice asks the Cheshire Cat for some assistance:

> *Alice: "Would you tell me, please, which way I ought to go from here?"*
>
> *The Cheshire Cat: "That depends a good deal on where you want to get to."*
>
> *Alice: "I don't much care where."*
>
> *The Cheshire Cat: "Then it doesn't much matter which way you go."*
>
> *Alice: "—so long as I get somewhere."*
>
> *The Cheshire Cat: "Oh, you're sure to do that if you only walk long enough."*[9]

If you want clients, peers, and your team to say "hell yes" to traveling eighty miles per hour in a forty-five mile per hour zone with you, meet them where they are. Get an appreciation for and understanding of their content and context. Meeting them where they are is key to winning their enrollment and engagement. Plus trust. Want them to get excited about the ride? Describe the opportunity and invite their perspective. As my client, let's call her Daniela, said to me, "It's all about communication, isn't it?"

Yes, Daniela, it is.

There's a great line from Dale Carnegie in his 1936 book, *How to Win Friends and Influence People*:

> *If there's any one secret of success, it lies in the ability to get the other person's point of view and see things from that person's angle as well as your own.*[10]

Most leaders think if they keep walking to get somewhere, their teams will follow because that's usually the natural order of things. Clients, peers, and teams will follow leaders who are excellent navigators or those who know the most efficient and optimal way to get from point A to point B.

Clarity, Like Sunlight, Is The Best Disinfectant

The biggest mistakes modern badasses make are based on the *assumption* that they have been clear to others about what they see as a goal or opportunity. Or the *assumption* that they have left enough breadcrumbs scattered about for other people to follow the trail. Or the *assumption* that they are the only ones with the right answers. Relying on assumptions can derail you.

Want to meet others where they are so they join the ride? Be your team's GPS. Clearly describe the opportunity and desired outcome as you see it in *their* content and context, in *their* language and terms. Badasses like you are a great reader of people *when* you are present and in the moment. Remember, your intuition game is strong. Allow that presence to guide the conversation.

Let them know they matter. You're smart enough to know what author Gay Hendricks calls your "Zone of Genius,"[11] the highest and best use of your time and talent, as well as how their Zone of Genius is complementary to yours. Effective badasses also know to have a values exploration to ensure those are in alignment as well. This is a key time to show them that what they do, how they do it, and who they are being are integral to a successful outcome. You know you won't be as successful without them. So why make this harder than it needs to be?

Your job as a visionary leader is not to be chief executive of everything. Instead, your job is to clarify the goal, invest in your people, recruit other great people, remind them why they are critical, and align the resources they need to maximize everyone's chances for success. Create the conditions for their success and get out of their way. *Their* success is *your* success.

Create A Goal GPS

You might not know how to construct a GPS that suits your purposes. Since you're a badass, it might be difficult for you to admit this. If this is true, I've outlined an approach you may wish to try.

Before you start, familiarize yourself with brainstorming techniques, because they will be the basis for creating your team GPS. Ideo, a design and consulting firm, offers these seven *ground rules*[12] for effective brainstorming sessions:

1. Defer judgment.
2. Encourage wild ideas.
3. Build on the ideas of others.
4. Stay focused on the topic.
5. One conversation at a time.
6. Be visual.
7. Go for quantity.

You'll have quickly noticed these rules are based on inclusion and not a rule of one. That's what's true for your objective too. Remember, you're not to be the chief executive of everything—sit back and let them shine. If you wish, you can scour the internet for more brainstorming rules too.

A Goal GPS Template

Think about your goal. Vividly. What does a successful goal accomplishment look like in one year or three years? What will you have created? What conditions did you and your team create to make it so? Who did you have to be as a leader to make it so? Who did they have to be as leaders to make it so?

Invite your team to a brainstorming session. Describe your goal as vividly as possible to your team, even making it multisensory if possible. Describe what the future looks like, the conditions that created the future state, and who you were as a leader to make it so. Couch this description in their terms and what you know to be their priorities, not yours.

Listen. Invite ideas, feedback, and questions. Don't listen for what seems most agreeable to you. Listen to everything. Ask about what they think of the goal and how they would stretch it. Check for resource constraints or guardrails like time, money, and human factors. Check for the "alerts" discussed in the previous chapter so you don't interrupt or derail the conversation. Ask what would make this goal rate eleven points out of a ten-point scale. Ask who they have to be as leaders to make the conditions maximize the possibility of a successful outcome.

Co-create the path forward. Choose the approach that best maximizes everyone's interests, passions, and talents. Establish a clear agreement regarding the goal and the approach to which everyone is committed. Also, establish an agreement to address times when there may be communication failures or disagreements about the path forward. This ensures everyone has "skin in the game," which is what the Dale Carnegie quote cited earlier in this chapter is really about.

Rinse. Repeat. This work is iterative, not one and done. You will always be more believable as a leader when you "open the floor to questions" and co-creation of opportunities.

Yes, Be Present

While you're having this conversation, be mindful that your confidence, energy, and excitement are served to motivate, not to intimidate or overwhelm. To aid you, you could invite a more senior leader on your team (or colleague) to moderate the conversation with you. Express your belief in what's possible when you are "all in" and committed to a shared goal. You could admit to your team that while you tend to Superman, you understand this is a time to resist that urge. You may even invite them to point it out to you when you're putting on the cape.

Also make it clear and easy to understand that their contributions and collective genius matter. You could even be a little edgy and say if they hold back a thought, they're stingy with their genius. Pick up on who may be holding back and invite them to participate on their terms, not yours. The more everyone leans into creativity and expertise, the more they have skin in the game. Even better, the more they feel they have skin in the game. This maximizes everyone's chances of success. You're creating a *partnership* based on a shared goal.

Dollars And Cents

That's the answer to the "Why bother?" question you might be thinking. Creating opportunities for everyone to have skin in the game is smart business sense. Inviting people into the dialogue and co-creating a shared goal maximizes your top and bottom lines.

Employee engagement is a key strategic initiative for every leader. Regarding employee disengagement, Gallup data estimates that actively disengaged employees cost the US $483 billion to $605 billion each year in lost productivity.[13] The annual global cost is about $8.1 trillion (USD).[14] Gallup data consistently shows that voluntary turnover costs US companies over one trillion dollars.[15]

Gallup data also shows that teams with talented managers enjoy a 48 percent increase in profitability, a 22 percent increase in productivity, and a 30 percent increase in employee engagement scores.[16]

It's tempting to believe that creating and nurturing clarity takes too long. That may be an effective strategy if you're running a sprint. But since you're in the long game, that ends up working against you. It's worth the effort, in other words.

Communicate. Communicate. Communicate. Invite dialogue. And then communicate some more. Create multiple opportunities to invite others' creativity to make the opportunity more expansive and accessible.

If this approach feels new to you, you're not alone. You will see that you accomplish what you believe is most important by being willing to hear what's most important to your team and clients first.

6

VULNERABILITY IS NOT A FOUR-LETTER WORD

Patrick Lencioni, bestselling author of *Getting Naked* and *Five Dysfunctions of a Team,* was right on the mark when he wrote this sentence:

> *When CEOs build real, deep, vulnerability-based trust with team members and understand the different contexts of conversations they are having, they can get the support they need while maintaining the authority their role requires.*[17]

Stephanie (true story, name changed) shared a great story about her first day in a role with higher visibility and consequently higher stakes than her previous roles. On that day, the CEO delivered a presentation to the team and she questioned the data he shared. Imagine ingesting a lot of risk, practically the size of an elephant, on your first day when you have zero goodwill stored in people's memory banks. It could be like asking for alienation, derision, and ridicule.

So what happened after Stephanie questioned him quite directly? The sky didn't fall. He accepted her point with grace at that moment because he wasn't focused on soothing his ego so much as he was on the big picture and wanted to model that for the team. For the rest of her time at the company, he continued asking for her perspective because she always spoke *truth to power* and he saw that as an asset, not an attack. That served him *and* the company well.

That exchange could have gone horribly wrong. At that moment, the CEO accepted where he was vulnerable, which was flawed data upon which he based conclusions. Stephanie chose to accept risk and speak up; he chose to listen instead of deflecting and hiding.

Many leaders believe they cannot or should not accept or display their vulnerability because it may diminish them in the eyes of others. The truth is that a veneer of invulnerability makes them less believable, less trustworthy, and therefore diminished.

If you struggle with appearing vulnerable, you're in excellent company. It's one of the hardest things for modern badasses to learn.

Be Seen As Human

Modern badasses invest a lot of time in *impression management,* creating a persona to boost their sense of authority or impermeability. It's more about the badass than the people around them. The desire to be and *look right all the time* is a highly addictive drug.

The suit of armor you've been wearing has been in place for so long, and it has often served you. It's understandable. You don't like to be caught not knowing something, or worse, caught with your proverbial pants down. It's embarrassing not to have 100 percent knowledge of a topic, all bases covered, or the *right* solution in hand at all times.

You might be motivated to appear strong and invulnerable. You love challenges—the harder, the better because you like to see how your solution affects everyone. What's good about leaders like you is that you're great strategic thinkers, quick on your feet, and have boundless energy. But it can feel *a bit much* and, candidly, isn't always believable. You might even appear (unintentionally) insufferable or smug.

There's a tremendous sense of horror and perceived risk in admitting vulnerability and insecurity. So it's a matter of survival for badasses to double down on appearing impermeable or even intimidating, rather like an oversized fig leaf. The thing is that the suit of armor and the decorative fig leaf work until they don't. People are smart and will pick up on your patterns, or at the very least, your energy. The more and longer you hide, the more you're exposed.

In other words, there's a significant business risk if you avoid appearing vulnerable and pay too little attention to the power of collaboration and community. Timothy Clark, CEO and founder of LeaderFactor, wrote:

After evaluating several agile teams and conducting a series of interviews with leading agile experts, I believe the primary factor is disregard for the first value of the Agile Manifesto: "Individuals and interactions over processes and tools."[18]

People trump strategy. People trump skill. People trump tools. Always.

Lead With Courage

Do you know what confidence is? The answer is that it is a lagging indicator of courage. In that story shared at the beginning of this chapter, both Stephanie and the CEO chose courage. She chose courage by assuming the risk of rejection in voicing her doubts. He chose courage by accepting his fallibility. Both modeled courage and vulnerability at that moment and each moment going forward.

What does leading with courage look like? Admit you know you don't know something. Ask for help. The phrase "fake it 'til you make it" sounds great on paper, but it's not a great long-term strategy. Elizabeth Holmes, the founder of Theranos, followed a "fake it" business strategy and even raised millions of dollars in investment from it. Her reward: criminal fraud conviction.

Consider Sara Blakely, founder of SPANX and a modern badass. She invented SPANX in the 1990s because she was frustrated with the limitations of women's undergarments. So a company was born with $5,000 and the salary she earned while selling fax machines door-to-door. This was despite her having no fashion, retail, or real business leadership experience. What she had plenty of, however, was courage. She cold-called high-end department stores, modeled her product during pitch meetings, and wouldn't let the possibility of failure be an excuse not to try even in the face of roadblocks. As she said in an interview:

> *It was extremely difficult for me to get the product made. I just kept hitting roadblock after roadblock. Nobody thought it was a good idea. I called a lot on the phone. I tried to make my own prototypes. I went to arts and crafts stores. That didn't really get me anywhere. I wasn't sure if the machine needed to be invented to create the product that I wanted to make. And it was like, how will I ever be able to afford that? I'm not an engineer. So there was a lot of self-doubt that was a roadblock for me in the beginning, but I ended up just persevering through those roadblocks by just not giving up. And I used a lot of persistence, balanced with humor, balanced with vulnerability, and I asked people to help. I wasn't afraid to say, look, I just need your help.*[19]

It's not that you don't feel fear. It's that you persist despite the fear, all the while believing that fear stands for "false evidence appearing real." And badasses like Blakely and you know there is an opportunity cost to sitting on the sidelines instead of pursuing an audacious goal. Blakely wrote on LinkedIn:

So many times, so many of us miss out on oppor-
tunities big and small because we are scared. It's
pretty easy to think about all the things that could
go wrong, and list all the reasons why not. We say
things to ourselves like, "I'm not good enough, that's
too hard, or I don't have the money, the experience
or the knowledge." But what if we just thought
about all things that could go right? What if instead
we could focus on all the amazing things that can
happen to us if we just had the courage to take the
leap? People ask me if I was scared when I started
@Spanx. Are you kidding? I was terrified. But the
thought of my life staying the way it was was scarier
to me than taking the risk. So if you're on the brink
of making a big decision that you know in your
heart is a good one, think about how your life will
expand. It's always possible that you will fall or
fail . . . but what if you fly?[20]

High-performing, super-driven leaders find it hard to
admit they don't know something or ask for help. They
believe making that admission is a sign of weakness that
puts undue pressure on them to figure it out, whether it's
in their Zone of Genius or not.

"Cultivate a network of trusted
mentors and colleagues. Other
people can give us the best insight
into ourselves—and our own
limitations. We must have the

courage to ask for help and to
request feedback to expand
our vision of what's possible."

—Maria Castañón Moats,
vice chair and assurance leader at
PricewaterhouseCoopers (PwC)[21]

Asking for help expands your vision of what's possible.
When you don't ask for help, it's like begging to have
blinders glued onto your head. In Kurt Vonnegut's excellent
short story *Harrison Bergeron*, one of the main characters
has above-average intelligence. The government makes him
wear a radio that regularly emits loud noises to interrupt
his thoughts to regulate his intelligence. Not asking for help
is exactly like that. You're creating your loud noises and
getting in the way of your intelligence.

You're leaving money on the table when you're not soliciting
ideas or feedback from your team. There's an opportunity
cost to not making the ask and an opportunity cost to
their silence.

Bluffing Only Works In Poker

As a leader, nothing is sacred, and that includes your ego.
Invite your peers and team into a conversation about possibilities. View their strengths as complementary to yours
rather than an indictment that you might be "weak" or
perceived as weak. In other words, channel their awesome
while channeling yours.

Don't be a prisoner of your expertise. Be open to learning new things or realizing where you may have made an unfounded assumption. Adam Grant, organizational psychologist and bestselling author, talks about how learning isn't about affirming beliefs so much as evolving them. In his book *Think Again: The Power of Knowing What You Don't Know* he says:

> *Rethinking is a skillset, but it's also a mindset. We already have the mental tools we need. We just have to remember to get them out of the shed and remove the rust.*[22]

Everything has a shelf life. There's only so much oomph in an idea, technology, or approach until it's replaced by something better. You improve as a leader when you accept that everything has a shelf life, including you.

Expertise can be cheeky, even a bit of a troll, because it feeds the ego and makes it believe it's more important than it is. The more we believe in the hype of our expertise, the more ego gets in the way of leading effectively and achieving our (moonshot) goals. And as I've mentioned in the Sixense Empathy Model, we know "Ego Kills Empathy."

Yes, even with a Growth Mindset, you can fall into cognitive entrenchment. It's possible to believe in constant learning but hold some ideas sacred. Realize that nothing is sacred to get a complete sense of what your strategic landscape could look like. Embracing that nothing is sacred means you get the best of everyone's genius, including yours.

Sixense Empathy Model

The Sixense Empathy Model helps you determine what's a symptom versus a problem. It assists in crystallizing issues and opportunities and helps make sense of all of the information. The Sixense Empathy Model empowers you to be ready to act on the results that drive success.

Y
YIELD TO THE MARKET
Don't fall in love with any ideas. Your customer has the final say. Meet your customers where they are and how they want to be delighted.

E
EGO KILLS EMPATHY
Leaders can be their own worst enemies. It's not about you. Start developing awareness for your people and your customers for better clarity and vision.

M
MAP YOUR PRESENT STATE
Where is your business today? Take stock of the unvarnished truth. There is no judgment or emotional attachment—just a "State of the State." You can't move forward without knowing where you are.

H
HONE YOUR APPROACH
Be open to learning from testing strategies and tactics. Implement changes and brainstorm new ideas to build on what is working. Trust in the process.

T
TEST NEW APPROACHES
Brainstorm ideas (strategies and tactics) to close the gaps between present and future. Document the process and results. Test – Learn – Test – Learn.

A
ASSESS THE GAP
You know where you are and you know where you want to be. What gaps or chasms need to be crossed to reach the future vision? Which gaps are priorities?

P
PLAN YOUR FUTURE STATE
What is possible? For your company, your customers, your people, and for you as a leader? Embrace the joy of possibility and paint a picture of what could be.

ANALYSIS / ACTION

The Crocodile Of Invulnerability Is Always Hungry

Since you're right frequently, you also get things wrong. That is the tragedy of the human condition. You will be wrong. A lot. Best get over it now than struggle with it forever. Admit you're fallible. People want to see you're human, not that you're perfect.

As Winston Churchill, the British prime minister during World War II, said:

> *Each one hopes that if he feeds the crocodile enough, the crocodile will eat him last.*[23]

This Churchill quote is often considered to be about appeasers. The more we try to appease, the less likely it will lead to a successful outcome. And that's true with the crocodile of invulnerability. The more audacious your goal, the more you need to starve the crocodile of invulnerability. The more you try to feed it, the more you'll be at odds with what you're trying to accomplish with and for your team, your clients, and yourself.

Brené Brown chose the title for her book *Dare Greatly* from a 1910 speech Theodore Roosevelt gave at the Sorbonne in Paris. Here's the part of the speech that still makes it important and memorable over one hundred years later:

> *It's not the critic who counts; not the man who points out how the strong man stumbles or where the doer of deeds could have done them better.*

The credit belongs to the man who is actually in the arena, whose face is marred by dust and sweat and blood; who strives valiantly . . . who at best knows the triumph of high achievement and who at the worst, if he fails, at least fails while daring greatly.

She has said in interviews that when she read the quote, she felt it represented vulnerability.[24] Her research shows vulnerability isn't a binary choice between winning or losing. Rather, it's understanding that both are necessary for all of us to be successful.

Essentially, being a modern badass means sharing all of you—not just the manufactured parts you wish others to see. It may be hard or even painful to develop this muscle, but it's critical for your growth as a leader. The more imperfect you admit you are, plus the more you seek the genius of others, the more influence you have as a leader. Wouldn't it be a relief to know you don't have to do it all yourself?

CONGRATULATIONS, YOU'RE HUMAN

You've won a lifetime supply of community and connection if you're willing to let go of being infallible and if you're willing to be seen as perfectly imperfect. Ask for help. Accept responsibility for mistakes you may have made. Be humble. Have a sense of humor when things go pear-shaped.

Until you get to that state of willingness, you'll continue to feed the crocodile of invulnerability. You'll likely be prone to make some unwise decisions to:

Double down on perfectionism. Perfectionism is a sure-fire way to burn out yourself and your team. It's also a highly effective way to alienate permanently the talented people you need most to accomplish the audacious goal you have in mind. The pursuit of perfection comes at the expense of the pursuit of knowledge and wisdom.

Try gaslighting on for size. As they say, denial is a river in Egypt. When you're unwilling to accept responsibility or the consequences, it's easier to make it seem like other people didn't have what it takes to succeed. It's always someone else's fault, and you're always the put-upon and long-suffering victim.

Wallow in self-blame and self-pity. You add to your negative highlight reel instead of learning from and applying what happened. It's constantly repeated in your head and is always available and hungry for more content. You also become more prone to victimhood.

Most people think it's the confidence you call on in those moments when you face your weakness and say it out loud. The truth is it's not confidence—it's courage. Courage comes first, and confidence comes later.

Facing your weakness can be a scary prospect, let alone ·saying it out loud. You're not alone if it seems like the hardest challenge you've ever had. You're not alone if you think it's probably better to put that armor back on instead of making what could seem like a humiliating admission. You're in excellent company in a very crowded room.

Be Seen As Human

You'll mess up. We all mess up. Frequently and royally. There's a line from the 1970 movie *Love Story*: "Love means never having to say you're sorry."

Tripe. Pure unadulterated tripe. Leadership means *requiring* us to accept and own responsibility for the small and large things we do. If we want the title and proverbial corner office, we must clean up our messes. The quicker you take responsibility, the faster you'll co-create a solution to a problem you've created or one you're facing as a leader. The quick acceptance of responsibility means a quick response from your team, peers, and colleagues along with their willingness to help.

President Richard Nixon learned during the Watergate crisis that the coverup is always worse than the crime. Lying, manipulation, and obfuscation make the error loom larger than it would if one just admitted to it. Ultimately, Nixon paid the price by making bigger and more serious mistakes to hide the first one. His legacy, perhaps, would have been a little less tarnished had he been honest and straightforward. The same holds true for the way British Prime Minister Boris Johnson tried to hide the cocktail parties he hosted at 10 Downing Street during the COVID-19 shutdown in the United Kingdom.

Rip Off The Band-Aid

There's a common infallibility belief leaders have that once they attain that title, almost as if they wear this belief like a force field. It's artificial and self-inflicted pressure that never yields anything productive. There's a tremendous opportunity cost that comes with that type of pressure—alienating others and missing the forest for the trees when it comes to leveraging resources and opportunity.

Say, "I need help" or "I'm sorry" or "I didn't realize that would happen." Yes, it's natural to be defensive the first few times. It's natural to feel insecure or uncertain. Saying it out loud makes it less weighty the sooner it's said out loud. Why carry a boulder on your back when you can have a pebble instead?

You can say something like the following:

"I caused _____. I accept responsibility. I see the impact on you/others/the project is _____. What I've learned from it is _____. Here's what I can commit to going forward: _____."

Or

"I need help with _____. I'm responsible for our team's shared success. I know I can't do it all, and I shouldn't do it alone, even though that's a default move and maybe even a bad habit. What do you think is missing? Who do you think we should include in this conversation?"

Actually, Love Does Mean Having To Say You're Sorry

There is an ancient Hawaiian practice called Ho'oponopono that blends love, forgiveness, gratitude, and repentance, intending to make things right or good.[25] It's known as a forgiveness prayer. While forgiveness certainly plays an important role, there's also an element of repentance, releasing negativity (and scarcity), and living more in abundance.

Ihaleakala Hew Len, a Hawaiian therapist, famously healed a ward of insane patients with his adaptation of Ho'oponopono without ever physically seeing them. He said, "I love you," "I am sorry," "Please forgive me," and "Thank you" repeatedly.

It's critical to note that forgiveness in this context is about forgiving yourself even if an outside actor harmed you. You're asking for help to forgive yourself for whatever you have that may have manifested the problem.

Forgiveness, like charity, starts at home. So does love.

Embrace Internal Disruption

Sometimes, whatever mode you've used to create disruption outside can be the same mode of disruption you create within. Internal disruption is what makes external disruption successful. The famous street artist Banksy was quoted in "The Art of Banksy" exhibit that toured the United States: "Think outside the box, collapse the box and take a f****** sharp knife to it."

You can think of all sorts of disruptive and change agent-y things. You can whiteboard, brainstorm, and edit like your life depends on it. That's a lot of fun. The thing is that is only half of the job.

The other half is to put your work out there to gauge reaction from others: good, bad, or indifferent. This means accepting that every reaction is perfect, even if it's a reaction you didn't want, including but not limited to failure. Disruption doesn't require confidence so much as it requires courage. An elevated leader accepts every outcome with grace and excitement. Each result helps direct you to where you can go next.

The disruption that remains in the proverbial lab to protect your ego is no disruption at all. It is, at best, a vanity project. The "being" of leadership commands you to step into larger, sometimes personally riskier, shoes in service of others.

Try Uncertainty On For Size

Uncertainty is often confused with imposter syndrome. They do not have the same meaning. Imposter syndrome is, "I hope they don't realize I don't belong here."

Uncertainty is simply that you're uncertain about the right path forward, how to get there, or from whom you ask for help.

Chuck Wisner, leadership advisor and author, wrote about the difference between the knower-versus-learner dynamic.[26] We are conditioned to be knowers or have the answer to everything. Badasses like you have a *knower* default. You feel compelled to know and be known for it.

When you lean on (false) certainty, your rooms get smaller over time, often without realizing it as it happens.

There's magic in learning how to be a *learner* instead. A learner can make things much easier and more expansive. A learner is humble and curious enough to ask questions when presented with uncertainty. An "I don't know" now creates discovery and opportunity later.

Wisner has offered tips to practice embracing uncertainty. The following are an extrapolation of those, provided to you as food for thought:

> ***Check your attitude at the door before going into a meeting or a challenging conversation.*** *The more you invite your ego into the room, the less able you will be to create connections with others. Practice active listening and be open to an idea exchange.*
>
> ***Investigate your emotions and your negative judgments.*** *Recall Adam Grant's words and wisdom about learning. The more we are open to learning, the better we accomplish shared goals.*
>
> ***Enter into conversations collaboratively.*** *This isn't a chance to compete. Not having an answer at the ready is to everyone's benefit. You don't have to speak first.*
>
> ***Don't overlook brainstorming creative conversations.*** *Use "Yes, and . . ." instead of "No,*

but . . ." to find common ground and even a better idea you would not have discovered on your own.

Slow down the decision-making process. *Recall Aesop's fable of the tortoise and the hare. Embracing slowness allows you to embrace more awareness. Slow and steady can win the race.*

Reframe uncertainty as a gift instead of a yoke. There is magic when you lean into ambiguity, which, as you know, is one of your favorite activities ever.

Stop Being Chief Executive Of Everything

There's a business case for seeking others' expertise. A December 15, 2020 article in *CEOWorld* entitled "4 Reasons Asking for Help Can Make You a More Effective Leader"[27] shared these benefits of being a hand-raiser:

More Informed Decisions. *Data shows that teams with diverse experiences make better decisions than individual decision-makers 87 percent of the time.*

Minimized Risk. *The echo chamber gets smaller and louder the less you seek the input and advice of your team and peers.*

Higher Employee Engagement and Morale. *Your people want to be respected for their skills and experiences. Allowing them to shine in their Zone of Genius creates alignment with the goal.*

Leadership Growth. *An excellent way to expand and grow as a leader is to ask for input and benefit from others' expertise.*

It just makes sense. You don't have to be the chief strategist and the person staffing your reception desk, virtual or otherwise. Cede control of executing the shared vision to those leaders on your team with the expertise needed to succeed and the passion to do that work. Free your time and attention to stay within your Zone of Genius as much as possible.

Dare Mighty Things

NASA's Mars Perseverance rover had that as a coded message in its parachute as it landed on the red planet. "Dare Mighty Things" is Jet Propulsion Laboratory's motto excerpted from the 1899 speech "Strenuous Life" delivered by Teddy Roosevelt.

> *"Far better is it to dare mighty things, to win glorious triumphs, even though checkered by failure . . . than to rank with those poor spirits who neither enjoy nor suffer much, because they live in a gray twilight that knows not victory nor defeat."*

Modern badasses, like all high performers, are scared of failure. Frequently. Every time you embrace risk, you may know victory or fail spectacularly. Regardless, you are compelled to lean into the challenge. It's your calling to do so. It's not confidence that makes you do this. It's courage. Your courage presents because you refuse to live in the gray twilight.

Accepting responsibility and fallibility is a refusal to live in the gray twilight. Pretending to be infallible is to embrace the gray twilight.

The temptation is great to appear impervious to anything. You're in good company when you do. However, you're playing a short game, not a long game, leaving money and opportunity on the table.

8

LATHER. RINSE. REPEAT.

One key point to make here is not that we're interested in creating a simple recipe to follow, like on the back of a grocery store cake mix. Adding water, oil, and an egg will not cut it when it comes to the work we are talking about.

The conversation has been and will be about you as a modern badass, fully in your expression and power so you can hit more and higher audacious goals, not compromising your values. The conversation also includes creating meaningful connections with others. You can enroll and engage others on your shared, larger goal. You might get so good at enrolling and engaging that you're an early recruit to a team because they know you're skilled at rallying the troops.

You're making an existential choice as to who you choose to be as a modern badass. You cannot turn a mighty lion into a docile sheep. You can work to create the conditions and environments where you present in the best light. You can redirect your energy and channel your considerable creativity, energy, and smarts.

Know the difference between mastery and performance. Mastery is a mindset of continued study, practice, and improvement. Think of mastery as velocity, which is the rate of travel in a given direction. Think of performance as speed, which is the rate of travel. Performance is a mindset fixated on a particular point in time.

The temptation is great for modern badasses to believe perfection is the point and pursue it relentlessly. The truth is that perfection isn't the point. Mastery is.

Getting In A Lather

Patrick (not his real name) had an epic meltdown, maybe even one for the ages. He had just engaged a consulting firm and the onboarding meeting wasn't going well. He didn't feel like the team understood him or his objectives. It felt like they were adding him to a premade, one-size-fits-all recipe instead of making one for his business needs. He lost it.

We had been working on some of the approaches shared in this book, and they went out the window when it was clear to Patrick that they weren't listening. To him, they weren't interested in creating a shared goal so much as treating him like a child who they put on leading strings. He had invested significant time and money in this project and could see failure looming on the horizon. The meeting ended poorly.

Afterward, when he had a chance to reflect, it hit him. Patrick fell out of alignment with his most important values, and it caused him to play a much smaller, more transactional game than he typically likes to play. He allowed fear of failure to influence his thoughts and consequently fell into a performance trap instead of pursuing mastery. He fell into the "Explosion" quadrant of the Values-Velocity Matrix.

"Getting in a lather" is an expression of getting upset about something. This type of lather gets modern badasses like us in trouble from time to time. You might get in a lather when you attempt some of the recommended approaches in this book with mixed results. You're a perfectionist, you don't like making mistakes, and you really don't like making very public mistakes. Nothing is worse than adding a mistake to your hall of fame.

When you let go of being right or always being the best, more learning and opportunity are available to you. Mastery is like the following Chinese philosopher Lao Tzu's gem from about 500 BCE:

> *When I let go of what I am,*
> *I become what I might be.*
> *When I let go of what I have,*
> *I receive what I need.*

Growth Mindset Is Your Friend

Belief in mastery goes hand in hand with having a growth mindset. Alan Kay, an American computer scientist and

TED speaker, coined the phrase, "The best way to predict the future is to invent it." We invite all of us to invent our futures as modern badasses. Developing and nurturing a growth mindset becomes very powerful for you. When we successfully create our futures, we're opening everyone up to the possibility of inventing their futures too.

Carol Dweck, the author of *Mindset: The New Psychology of Success,* has devoted herself to studying what makes people successful and what factors play into that success. She says mindsets are theories we create about ourselves.

Dweck's popular work focuses on two mindsets: fixed and growth. The former is the belief that your qualities are unchangeable and you're more motivated to be right or perfect than to learn. A fixed mindset means that you have an emotional attachment to finding an outcome that always puts you in the best light, like impression management. Fixed mindset leaders plateau earlier than they should because they've narrowed the playing field to only where they can be perfect. It can feel like limiting your peripheral vision.

In Dweck's book, she mentions leaders having a fixed mindset in the form of what she called CEO disease:

> *Speaking of reigning from atop a pedestal and wanting to be seen as perfect, you won't be surprised that this is often called "CEO disease." Lee Iacocca had a bad case of it. After his initial success as head of Chrysler Motors, Iacocca looked remarkably like our four-year-olds with the fixed mindset. He kept*

> *bringing out the same car models over and over*
> *with only superficial changes. Unfortunately, they*
> *were models no one wanted anymore.*[28]

Those of us who remember how Japanese cars dominated the market in the 1980s can tell you that Chrysler's approach neglected the changing landscape and demands of the consumer. A fixed mindset did not allow Iacocca or Chrysler's leadership to see how it would be in their and their stockholders' best interest if they were to yield to the market to remain competitive. Perhaps a more contemporary example would be how Blackberry miscalculated iPhone novelty and popularity, how Netflix and Amazon films have upended the motion picture and television industry, or even how streaming has disrupted the cable industry.

A growth mindset is based on the belief that talents develop continuously. Being right is never the point, but learning is. You tend to be more successful if you have a growth mindset because you love to learn, don't care about looking smart, and aren't emotionally attached to an outcome.

Learning and stretching with a growth mindset is a craving. Dweck also wrote:

> *People in a growth mindset don't just seek chal-*
> *lenge, they thrive on it. The bigger the challenge,*
> *the more they stretch. And nowhere can it be seen*
> *more clearly than in the world of sports. You can*
> *just watch people stretch and grow.*[29]

Love him or not, Michael Jordan, retired Chicago Bulls basketball player and six-time NBA world champion, is the perfect embodiment of a growth mindset, a modern badass, and a 3D leader. Jordan was a diligent and disciplined student of his competitors, often watching recordings of their games to see how he could leverage his strength and minimize his weaknesses against them. During his playing years, and especially during the threepeat championship wins, he was often the first to the gym and the last to leave.

Furthermore, as his body started to age, he found new ways to dominate the game of basketball and master basketball strategy. For him, it was about new ways to master his ever-changing body. He loved the challenge of it, and it showed.

He loved to win and that drive worked both for him and against him. His passion, however, was and still is palpable to this day. It's hard to argue with his record. He got the job done.

The Power Of Yet

Yet is the favorite word of a growth mindset leader. A growth mindset leader never counts themselves out. They intuitively know they will achieve what they see in their mind's eye, even if it's not immediately clear what the exact path to success is. It's not if they will get there—it's that they haven't gotten there *yet*. Or as attributed to Thomas Edison:

> *I have not failed 10,000 times. I have successfully found 10,000 ways that will not work.*

A growth mindset leader knows that individual performances are not the objective as much as mastery is. They are always in the process of passionately inventing their futures.

The belief in the power of yet keeps them detached from individual outcomes in favor of the overarching goal. So while Michael Jordan may have missed an individual shot in a game, he knew another shot would be available.

Growth mindset leaders know how to channel creativity, energy, and smarts. What if the consequences of channeling your creativity, energy, and smarts in a new way exceeded your expectations of what was possible? Leaning into a desire to iterate and iterate again creates more opportunities for all of us.

Badass, you know how to thrive even in the most challenging times. Don't let the performance, fixed-mindset troll distract you from being the mastery-oriented, growth- mindset leader you can be.

You Might Be Resistant

If you're worried about embracing a change in approach, that's natural and understandable. You've worn the mantle of Superman instead of Clark Kent for so long that it will feel weird to make that switch. But knowing you're a modern badass, you've got some pretty audacious things in mind that will compel you to step into courage, if not confidence, to do what you've set out to do. Helen Keller wrote:

> *Life is either a daring adventure or nothing. To keep our faces toward change and behave like free spirits in the presence of fate is strength undefeatable.*[30]

The choice is yours at this moment. Do you head toward change or keep choosing the same behaviors, hoping for completely different results?

The extent of your strength and impact as a leader is a choice that is always available to make. You can choose to be the one who makes the donuts or choose to be the one who makes new donut recipes. The former maintains the status quo and the latter keeps a courageous face toward change.

To be clear, a mindset alone isn't enough. You need that, plus concrete tools, approaches, and tips to help support you in your mastery journey. If you find this difficult to pursue, remember that time spent focusing on mastery and embracing a growth mindset is always like finding money, like discovering a $20 bill in your favorite pair of jeans after you've done the laundry.

9

THE GOLDILOCKS EFFECT

"Goldilocks and the Three Bears" is a famous children's story. In the story, Goldilocks enters a home without permission and samples porridge, the various chairs, and all its beds. When she samples three bowls of porridge, she determines the porridge in the first bowl is too hot, the porridge in the second bowl is too cold, and the porridge in the third bowl is just right. She then went on to learn which of the three chairs and which of the three beds were just right for her too.

The term *The Goldilocks Effect* was borne of research on how infants approach decision-making.[31] The lead scientists of the University of Rochester–sponsored study focused on how infants make sense of a world that is full of multiple and often complex sights, sounds, and movements. The research data showed that infants pay little attention to information that's simple or complex, preferring instead to have situations that contain just the right amount of surprise or complexity for them.

In the spirit of The Goldilocks Effect, modern badass leaders are not too anything. They can be and are just right for every situation or project.

It would be understandable if you were to believe this book should have been titled *I Love You, You're Perfect, Now Change.* as a wink and a nod to the long-running, successful off-Broadway musical by the same name. The truth is that it would be a complete waste of time and talent for you to change. It would also be a short-sighted fool's errand for other people to try to change you.

You Define Your Leadership In Each Moment

One of the things I notice most in my self-styled field of modern badass anthropology is that it has been easy, actually preferred, to dismiss or disempower modern badasses with the word "too" used to describe them. "Too much," "too fast," or "too disruptive" may be how you've heard descriptions of yourself. It's easier for people to sideline you than it is for them to try to meet you where you are. In the children's story, it was easier for Goldilocks to take what wasn't hers than it was for her to practice a little environmental awareness.

Your leadership is defined moment by moment and not in a laboratory where you're outfitted in a hazardous materials suit. Given whatever you believe your legacy to be, it's of the utmost importance for you to engage and enroll others as to what you believe possibility is for everyone, not just you.

No, it doesn't mean you compromise who you are or your values. Rather, it means allowing people to have a glimpse of your why, your mission, and your purpose so that you, your values, and your passions are better understood.

Why now? People leave leaders; they don't leave companies, nor do they leave jobs. If you don't feel appreciated by either your peers or the powers that be, they're leaving money on the table. Similarly, if neither your peers nor your team have a handle on what you see as opportunity, they will also walk. And that means you'll be leaving money on the table. There is an emotional cost to disengagement and a high hard dollar cost to it too.

What Is Required Of You

Courage is an excellent first step for you to call on as you embark on your next audacious goal. You often find yourself in a situation where all you have is an interesting idea and courage because you lean into having a growth mindset and learning. Some adventures may seem harder or riskier than others, but as a general matter, you know that you have the capacity to climb steep learning curves.

The thing with courage, however, is that if you're not careful, it can be treated transactionally. Specifically, you can have the courage to bungee jump just one time. Or you can have the courage to jump out of a plane just one time. You can also run the risk of getting bored quickly. There are so many times you can bungee jump, for example, before the novelty of it can wear off and you decide something else seems more interesting.

What your legacy requires of you as a modern badass leader is an attribute that is a little bit more nuanced or complex, like an excellent coffee or a glass of wine. Strength is what is required. Here are some elements that can build your strength as a leader:

Courage. This is the ability to do something that scares us. For you, it may be like JFK's moonshot mission in your pursuit of something that is so "out there" that few of us can envision it. Or it could be leaving your corporate life behind and giving yourself permission to pursue a startup idea you've had for a long time. You move ahead even though you may be experiencing fear.

Conviction. This represents your belief that what you're doing is right, just, and aligned with who you are and what your values are. In other words, you're firmly ensconced in the upper right "Excellence" box of the Values-Velocity Matrix. You know what you're doing is what you're meant to be doing now and moving forward, come hell or high water.

Sustainability. This means you have and will devote the energy, the will, the commitment, the intention, the desire, and the endurance to go for this for the long haul, even if you face some naysayers and doubters. You are in the daily and regular practice of sharing what you do and why you do what you do so you enroll and engage those around you.

Belief. Different from conviction, this is your belief in yourself and your unique gifts. This is your belief that you can do what you're being called to do and your belief in the value you bring to the table for everyone's benefit in the near and long term. Within this belief resides an ability to identify the triggers of imposter syndrome and uncertainty as well as the determination to beat them back to get to what you see is possible in your mind's eye.

You Might Regress

Yes, you might regress. You may really shine in some elements of your badassery and yet still struggle in other elements. The Goldilocks Principle, remember, is about being just right, not perfect.

Regression is actually an excellent sign. It can show us where we are growing and not growing in stark relief. It can show us where we are susceptible to some lingering bad habits that get in the way of what is possible. Remember, as a growth mindset leader, you believe every outcome is perfect.

Here is an excerpt from an article by Kristin Hendrix:

> *We can either master our ego, or it can master us. We absolutely must have confidence in our ability . . . whether it's to do the job at hand, make an informed decision, or lead a team through change. At the same time, we must also have awareness of our limitations. There are universal truths that every leader eventually learns. Hopefully not the hard way.*[32]

Audacious goals are killed by our ego. The gift of leadership is knowing what our Zone of Genius is and how to stay in it. This knowledge makes it easier for us to recognize we need help and then ask for it.

The urge to be perfect, at least appear so, is understandable, but the truth is that it makes us stagnate rather than progress. The more you say "I'm stuck" or "Can you help me?" the more powerful of a voice you have. No one is obligated to be your mind reader or deduce that you may need their assistance. If you can't say what you specifically need and why you may need it, no one will do the heavy lifting for you.

Remember that the best leaders create teams that complement them, not mirror them. Know your gifts and cultivate an organization that can add to them so you can confidently raise your hand and ask for that help. Your team is your strategic feedback loop.

Reality TV is the only place you win a $1 million solo survivor prize. Do yourself a favor and shed that armor of perfection. It's gotten too heavy and it does nothing for your figure. Remember that you're more of a badass when you ask for help instead of assuming the mantle of chief executive of everything.

Your Legacy Is Calling

In Shakespeare's play *Julius Caesar*, Mark Antony delivers the eulogy during Caesar's funeral and these two lines in his speech seem apt to remind you of:

> *The evil that men do lives after them;*
> *The good is oft interred with their bones.*

Let's make it so that what you are called to do, what you accomplish, and your good lives after you and whatever perceived evil are interred or better yet, forgotten instead. The way good lives after you is by establishing content and context through connection and understanding, not by trying to change you or the person sitting on the other side of the table. And not by the person sitting on the other side of the table trying to change you, either.

Your legacy is calling. It's up to you to answer.

10

HUGGING A CACTUS

This book started off with a painful and personal story about my leadership travails as a fellow modern badass and 3D leader. I've been told I'm too aggressive, brash, and bold. I've been told I alienate some people and intimidate others. I've been told I am difficult. Working with me, to hear others describe it, was like trying to hug a cactus.

My journey continues as a traveler alongside you and maybe in some cases, a few steps ahead of you. Previously, I understood power but only in a super raw form. I knew how to speak truth to power but whether I was seen or heard is a completely different story altogether. The challenge was deploying the right amount of power at the right strategic time so I could be seen as influential. This is your challenge too.

I have learned and believe this challenge was a gracious invitation to me. And it's also a gracious invitation to you. You deserve to be, act, and celebrate in the best expression of your influence if you choose to accept the invitation extended to you throughout this book.

You Have An Invitation To Blossom

The invitation to blossom is really an invitation for you to take a look in the mirror and explore, non-judgmentally, what happened in the past so you can write your impactful future. Explore your most valuable lessons, glean some insights, and understand the impact of those insights not only for your own benefit but for those around you too.

In my case, I started to blossom when I realized I didn't have clarity on the degree of my force or power, what my key values are, why my key values mattered, and what types of environments are best suited for who I am as a person and a leader. I also started to understand the link between a lack of clarity and everything it has cost me in my career.

Blossoming happens for every modern badass when they know their values and how to stay in alignment with them. They also blossom when they know the difference between their form of speed versus velocity as well as how to redirect back to velocity when they accidentally fall into speed.

What's At Stake

How badly do you want to blossom? What makes you a modern badass is your potential to have an outsized impact on your community once you see how it is that you get in your own way and then construct the means to stop doing that. And that's the key, once you see how it is that you get in your own way.

Leaning into this invitation to blossom means you lean into developing more environmental awareness not only so you drive more results but to be seen as a believable and trustworthy leader. Imagine what it would be like for you if you were seen as an indispensable and influential leader as opposed to a leader others would rather sideline and silence because it just feels "easier" to do so. We know how painful it is to be sidelined and so the question to you is what you're willing to do to not repeat the experience.

Your genius is also at stake. You have a unique gift and unique voice to share with the world. And the world should see the best use of your time and talent so everyone can benefit.

How Does This Get Done?

The best use of your time and talent is in being multi-lingual: an appreciated valuable disruptor on the outside while channeling and translating your awesome for those on the inside. Here is a refresher on how you can get this done.

Build community. You may not know it or see it, but you have people around you who will champion you if you allow them access to your real (or proverbial) laboratory. People aren't mind readers. So they need a glimpse of what's possible so they can be just as excited about the adventure as you are. They also want to feel like you will allow them to help you shine. Don't be selfish. Let them do it.

Share your values. A shared understanding begins by sharing what is most sacred to you: your values. Explain what they are and why they are so important. Your willingness to share will prompt others to share their values and why they are so important too. What follows is a way to meet in the middle instead of what can feel like a very tense turf war that wastes time, effort, and energy.

Choose velocity, not speed. Speed is solely the rate of travel. Velocity is the rate of travel in a given direction. Velocity is what having a clearly defined goal looks like. When you move quickly, your colleagues, teams, and clients are more apt to move as fast as you when they have a clear picture of the goal in mind. Your responsibility as a visionary is to create the ideal conditions for velocity and recognize when you may be reverting to the bad habit of speed instead.

Be inefficient. It's tempting to believe that meeting people where they are will be inefficient and slow everything down. It feels right to go it alone every time and often feels easier not to have to explain everything or map out the path to success. You might even call that the efficient approach to achieving your goals. The truth is that it is wildly inefficient when you sacrifice a broader strategic landscape by not inviting other people's perspectives and experiences into your planning. The tortoise won the race in Aesop's fable and yet he was much slower than the hare.

Get naked. Not literally. Patrick Lencioni's book *Getting Naked*[33] is popular and for very good reason. Admitting that you're not an expert or you don't have the skills to be an expert is like drinking a glass of cold water on a hot, sticky, and humid day. It's a relief to let go of being chief executive of everything. Dump that suit of armor. It's not your color. People are wise and know that the more you wear the armor, the more obvious your weaknesses are. Your bravado fools no one.

Make frequent mistakes. Along with dumping that suit of armor, dump the belief that you have to get it right the first time, every time. You also don't have to be the first one to the finish line, either. Take a backseat and let the collective genius of your peers and team shine. No one likes a know-it-all, least of all you. Make some messes. Draw some crooked lines. Spill some milk. The more you show your fallibilities and your vulnerabilities, the more relatable and believable you are as a leader.

It's mastery, not perfection. The beauty of being a modern badass like you is also what might hold you back. You're so eager to put your vision out into the world for everyone to enjoy. And you're upset that it may take a few attempts to get there. Or you may learn it doesn't work at all. Remember that every outcome is perfect because it gives you information as to what you could do next. You're not a "one and done" leader. The intersection of experimentation and iteration is where possibility lives.

A State Of Being

Being a modern badass leader isn't an end state. It's a state of being and a state of mind. You are and always will be a pattern interrupter and change agent called to serve the greater good for everyone, whether they can appreciate you or not. The degree, duration, and sustainability of your impact, your legacy, is 100 percent within your control. How do you choose to channel your awesome?

As Steve Jobs, a modern badass leader, narrated in the "Think Different" commercial:

> *People who are crazy enough to think they can change the world are the ones who do.*

I believe in you, badass. You have more impact, potential, and power than you know because you can be crazy enough to believe and think you can change the world.

I enjoy my blossom more when I see yours in its fullest color and expression. What are you waiting for?

APPENDIX

Acknowledgments

This book wouldn't be possible without all the modern badasses and 3D leaders who have so much to give and yet don't always feel understood. I see you even if we've never met. Thank you for being so committed and not compromising your principles and values.

I am grateful to the 4PC Community. We've all agreed that we can't ever get too big or too messy, and these lovely souls have seen a lot of my mess up close. Thank you for your magic.

Thanks to Rich Litvin. It seems too simple to call him my coach; he has helped me locate the portals for all my current magic and the magic to come from me. Thank you for your friendship, humanity, and kindness.

Much gratitude to my editor, Henry DeVries. I can't begin to count the number of times Henry has challenged and championed me as a wise book coach and editor on this adventure. Thank you for being my beacon.

Thanks to my sounding board. I have lost count of the times I've expressed anxiety and second-guessed myself to Dina and Shelley. Thank you for seeing me and loving me as I am.

Thanks to my informal editors, David, Elaine, Hayden, and Sarah. Thank you for the input and the love.

Much appreciation and gratitude to and for Roya Behnia. She is my big sister, whom I still look up to (even though I'm taller), and my first steadfast cheerleader. Thank you for your consistent love and loyalty.

Where would I be without Alieh and Rahim Behnia? My parents created a life for me so that I could shine. Thank you for loving me unconditionally and only ever wishing for my happiness and well-being.

And of course, Amir Homayoun Rafizadeh. This adventure wouldn't have been possible had he not told me to "unleash the beast" and join 4PC, let alone his continued faith and support in me as a leader and a person. Thank you for loving me and telling me it's okay, actually needed, for me to roar.

About The Author

PARISSA BEHNIA coaches C Suite and senior leaders who are high-will, high-skill and have a growth mindset. In other words, they're badasses like you who go eighty miles per hour in a forty-five mile per hour zone but don't always check to see if their team is strapped in or interested in going for the ride. These leaders are of high value to a company but their edges may start to diminish their value.

These days, leadership is full of complexities, whether you're navigating from an audacious goal or trying to avoid that iceberg up ahead. In either case, Parissa's clients choose her because she's either sat in those seats or next to those seats often enough to know how it can feel to be alone in a crowded leadership room. She's unafraid to speak truth to power and help propel you forward.

With over twenty years of corporate, consulting, coaching, and—let's be honest—real-life experience, Parissa's key strategic difference is empathy. Empathy in business is more than being nice to one another; it's a strategic imperative. It means that leaders seek content and context to do a better job of serving their customers *and* engaging their teams. She's so passionate about employing empathy in business that she's developed the Sixense Empathy Model. And she wants all of us to put empathy at the forefront of how we engage with everybody.

One of Parissa's favorite things to do is to stand in front of a whiteboard—real or pretend—to help clients imagine what the world could look like and then propel them as they navigate to that vision of success. This work enables clients to put together pieces of the puzzle to create the aha moment that ignites action. She leans into the discomfort of the unknown and invites her clients to embrace all their talents (even ones they don't recognize or value fully) to create their own paths to success.

Parissa has taught entrepreneurship seminars and is a frequent speaker on strategy, leadership, and entrepreneurship. She is a Certified Professional Coach and holds a BA from Northwestern University and MBA from NYU's Stern School of Business.

Notes

1 Gabriel Sherman, "'You Don't Bring Bad News To The Cult Leader': Inside The Fall of WeWork," *Vanity Fair*, https://www.vanityfair.com/news/2019/11/inside-the-fall-of-wework, November 21, 2019.

2 Brené Brown, *The Gifts of Imperfection* (Minnesota: Hazelden Publishing, 2010).

3 Sunny Bonnell and Ashleigh Hansberger, *Rare Breed*, (New York: HarperOne, 2019).

4 Albert Einstein, *Life* magazine, May 2, 1955.

5 "The Nine Enneagram Type Descriptions," The Enneagram Institute, https://www.enneagraminstitute.com/type-descriptions.

6 Email Interview with Hayden Lee, March 8, 2022.

7 Jordan Goldrich, *Workplace Warrior: People Skills For The No-Bullshit Executive,* (Austin, TX: Greenleaf Book Press, 2019)

8 Mary Bagley, "Mount Vesuvius & Pompeii: Facts & History," Live Science, December 19, 2017, https://www.livescience.com/27871-mount-vesuvius-pompeii.html.

9 Lewis Carroll, *Alice in Wonderland* (London: Macmillan, 1865).

10 Dale Carnegie, *How to Win Friends and Influence People* (New York: Simon & Schuster, 1936).

11 Gay Hendricks, *The Big Leap* (New York: HarperOne, 2010).

12 "7 Simple Rules of Brainstorming," Ideo U, https://www
.ideou.com/blogs/inspiration/7-simple-rules-of-brainstorming.

13 State of the American Workplace: 2017 Report, Gallup.

14 State of the Global Workplace: 2021 Report, Gallup.

15 Shane McFeely and Ben Wigert, "This Fixable Problem Costs
U.S. Businesses $1 Trillion," Gallup, https://www.gallup.com
/workplace/247391/fixable-problem-costs-businesses-trillion
.aspx, March 13, 2019.

16 Adam Hickman, Ph.D., "Why Manager Development Is A
Top Goal For Leaders This Year," Gallup, January 1, 2020,
https://www.gallup.com/workplace/272171/why-manager
-development-top-goal-leaders-year.aspx.

17 Patrick Lencioni, "For CEOs, Loneliness Is Not An Option,"
ChiefExecutive, https://chiefexecutive.net/for-ceos-loneliness
-is-not-an-option/, May 18, 2021.

18 Timothy R. Clark, "Agile Doesn't Work Without Psychological
Safety," *Harvard Business Review,* February 21, 2022, https://hbr
.org/2022/02/agile-doesnt-work-without-psychological-safety.

19 "From Selling Fax Machines to Becoming The Youngest
Self-Made Female Billionaire: A Conversation with CEO and
Spanx Founder Sara Blakely," Blazing Trails Podcast, Salesforce
Studios, October 28, 2020, https://podcasts.salesforce.com
/public/38/Blazing-Trails-561264f7/fcc7252e.

20 Sara Blakely, Linkedin.com, https://www.linkedin.com/posts
/sarablakely27_courage-fear-adventure-activity-6826518980
468056064-2Ra7?utm_source=linkedin_share&utm_medium
=member_desktop_web

21 Jen Luciani, "28 Powerful Women Share Their Best Advice,"
Shape, https://www.shape.com/celebrities/interviews/28
-powerful-women-share-their-best-advice, August 13, 2013.

22 Adam Grant, *Think Again: The Power of Knowing What You
Don't Know* (New York: Viking Press, 2021).

23 "The War Situation: House of Many Mansions," International
Churchill Society, https://winstonchurchill.org/resources
/speeches/1940-the-finest-hour/the-war-situation-house
-of-many-mansions/.

24 Dan Schawbel, "Brené Brown: How Vulnerability Can Make Our Lives Better," *Forbes*, April 21, 2013, https://www.forbes .com/sites/danschawbel/2013/04/21/brene-brown-how -vulnerability-can-make-our-lives-better/?sh=6e05900f36c7.

25 "Ho'oponopono: The Hawaiian Miracle Healing Prayer For Peace, Forgiveness, Health, Wealth & Happiness," Ho'oponopono Miracle, https://hooponoponomiracle.com /ho-oponopono-hawaiian-forgiveness-prayer/.

26 Chuck Wisner, "How Leaders Can Unwrap The Gift of Uncertainty," SmartBrief On Leadership, April 1, 2021, https://www.smartbrief.com/original/2021/04/how-leaders -can-unwrap-gift-uncertainty.

27 Ann Dieleman, "4 Reasons Asking For Help Can Make You A More Effective Leader," CEOWORLD, https://ceoworld .biz/2020/12/15/4-reasons-asking-for-help-can-make-you-a -more-effective-leader, December 15, 2020.

28 Carol Dweck, *Mindset: The New Psychology of Success* (New York: Ballantine Books, 2006).

29 Dweck, Mindset, 2006.

30 Helen Keller, *Let Us Have Faith* (New York: Doubleday, 1944).

31 "The Goldilocks Effect: Babies Learn From Experiences That Are Not Too Simple, Not Too Complex, But 'Just Right'," University of Rochester, May 23, 2012, https://www.rochester .edu/news/show.php?id=4071.

32 Kristin Hendrix, "Why Ego Can Be A Leader's Greatest Strength And Their Downfall," LeadershipVitae, April 8, 2021, https://leadershipvitae.com/2021/04/why-ego-can-be -a-leaders-greatest-strength-and-their-downfall/.

33 Patrick Lencioni, *Getting Naked: A Business Fable About Shedding the Three Fears That Sabotage Client Loyalty* (Hoboken, NJ: Jossey-Bass, 2010).

Milton Keynes UK
Ingram Content Group UK Ltd.
UKHW051122091023
430203UK00010B/64

9 781957 651217